WEATHER
Infographics

Chris Oxlade

Raintree is an imprint of Capstone Global Library Limited, a company incorporated in England and Wales having its registered office at 7 Pilgrim Street, London, EC4V 6LB – Registered company number: 6695582

www.raintreepublishers.co.uk
myorders@raintreepublishers.co.uk

Edited by Rebecca Rissman, Dan Nunn, and John-Paul Wilkins
Designed by Philippa Jenkins
Original illustrations © Capstone Global Library Ltd 2014
Illustrations by HL Studios
Picture research by Elizabeth Alexander
Production by Vicki Fitzgerald
Originated by Capstone Global Library Ltd
Printed and bound in China

ISBN 978 1 406 27212 3
17 16 15 14 13
10 9 8 7 6 5 4 3 2 1

British Library Cataloguing in Publication Data
Oxlade, Chris.
Weather. – (Infographics)
A full catalogue record for this book is available from the British Library.

Acknowledgements
We would like to thank the following for permission to reproduce photographs: Capstone Global Library p. 4; Shutterstock pp. 4 (© M.Stasy, © Pakhnyushcha, © Stella Caraman, © Thomas Bethge), 8 (© Alhovik), 9 (© Smit).

We would like to thank Diana Bentley and Marla Conn for their invaluable help in the preparation of this book.

Every effort has been made to contact copyright holders of any material reproduced in this book. Any omissions will be rectified in subsequent printings if notice is given to the publisher.

Disclaimer
All the internet addresses (URLs) given in this book were valid at the time of going to press. However, due to the dynamic nature of the internet, some addresses may have changed, or sites may have changed or ceased to exist since publication. While the author and publisher regret any inconvenience this may cause readers, no responsibility for any such changes can be accepted by either the author or the publisher.

CONTENTS

About infographics 4

What is weather? 6

Temperature 8

Types of weather 10

Clouds 16

Extreme weather 20

Climates 24

Weather forecasting 28

Glossary................................ 30

Find out more 31

Index 32

Some words are shown in bold, **like this**. You can find out what they mean by looking in the glossary.

ABOUT INFOGRAPHICS

An infographic is a picture that gives you information. Infographics can be graphs, charts, maps, or other sorts of pictures. The infographics in this book are about weather.

Infographics make information easier to understand. We see infographics all over the place, every day. They appear in books, in newspapers, on the television, on websites, on posters, and in adverts.

Weather for the week

Here is an example of a weather infographic. It shows what the weather might be like for the next week in a particular place.

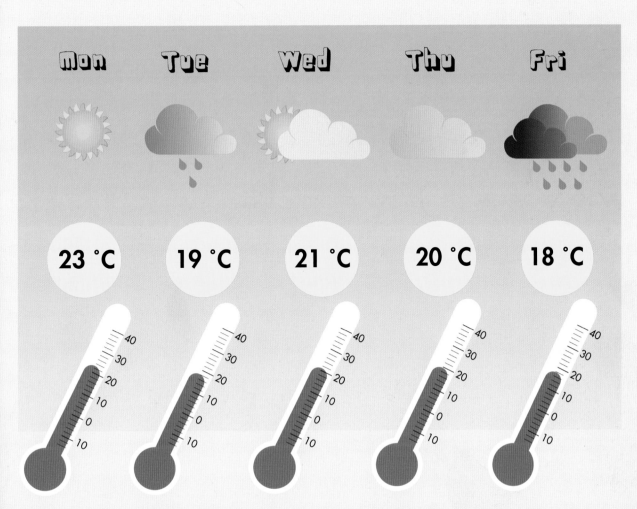

WHAT IS WEATHER?

Weather can be sunny or cloudy, wet or dry, warm or cold, or windy or **calm**. It can also be a mixture of lots of these things! We use different symbols to show different types of weather.

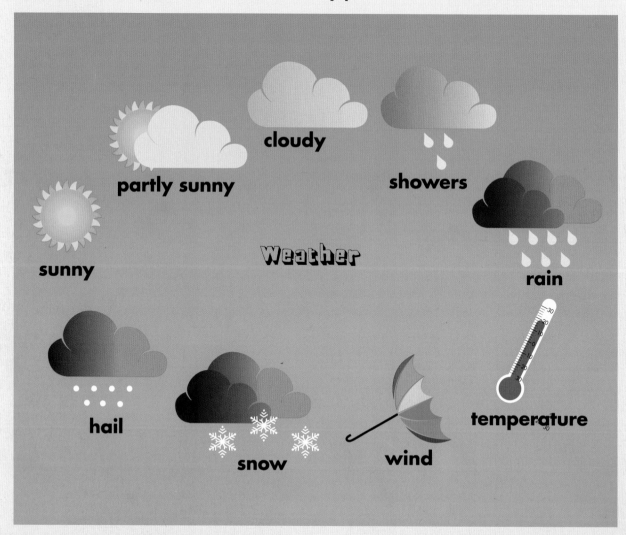

cloudy

showers

partly sunny

sunny

rain

Weather

hail

snow

wind

temperature

World record weather

Some places in the world are very hot or very cold. Some are very wet and some are very dry. Some are very windy. This map shows some world-record weather around the world.

Sunniest place on Earth
Yuma, Arizona, USA
11.4 hours of sunshine per day on **average**

Hottest place on Earth
Death Valley, California, USA
56.7 °C (highest)

Wettest place on Earth
Mawsynram, India
1,187 centimetres of rain per year

Driest place on Earth
Arica, Chile
0.8 millimetres of rain per year

Coldest place on Earth
Vostock, Antarctica
−89.2 °C (lowest)

Windiest place on Earth
George V Coast, Antarctica
320 kilometres per hour

TEMPERATURE

How warm today?

Weather experts record the **temperature** regularly through the day and night. This is an example of a 24-hour temperature record. It shows how hot or cold it was every 3 hours from midday on 1 February to midday on 2 February in 2012, in Pittsburgh, USA.

Temperature in degrees Celsius

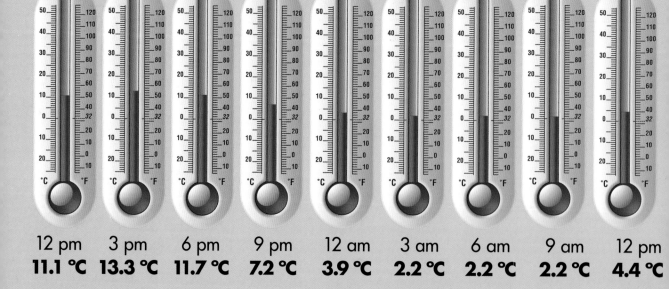

12 pm	3 pm	6 pm	9 pm	12 am	3 am	6 am	9 am	12 pm
11.1 °C	**13.3 °C**	**11.7 °C**	**7.2 °C**	**3.9 °C**	**2.2 °C**	**2.2 °C**	**2.2 °C**	**4.4 °C**

How warm this week?

Weather experts record the weather all over the world every day. This graph shows the **average** temperature in London on each day for a week in September 2012.

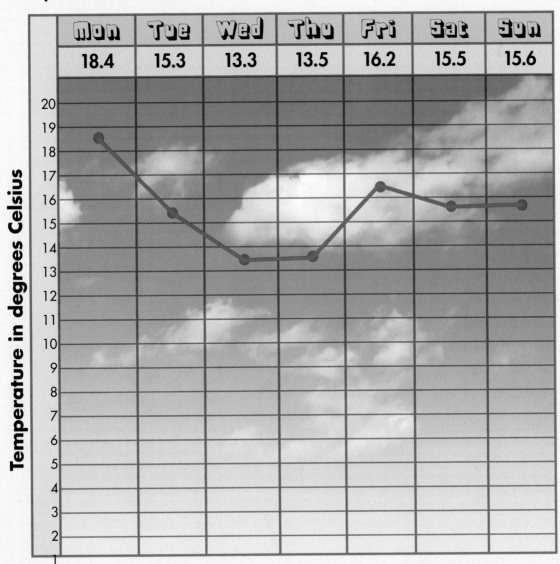

Mon	Tue	Wed	Thu	Fri	Sat	Sun
18.4	15.3	13.3	13.5	16.2	15.5	15.6

TYPES OF WEATHER

How much rain this week?

This is an example of a weekly rainfall chart. It shows how much rain fell each day for a week.

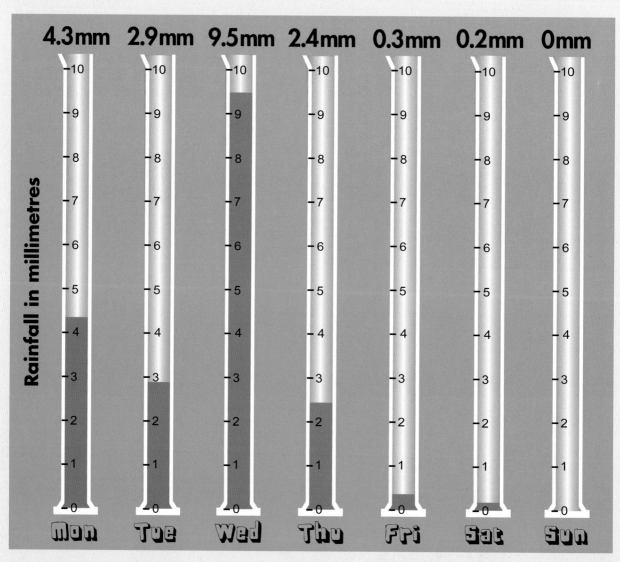

4.3mm	2.9mm	9.5mm	2.4mm	0.3mm	0.2mm	0mm
Mon	Tue	Wed	Thu	Fri	Sat	Sun

Rainfall in millimetres

The heaviest rain
Sometimes it rains very heavily indeed. This chart shows some of the heaviest downpours ever.

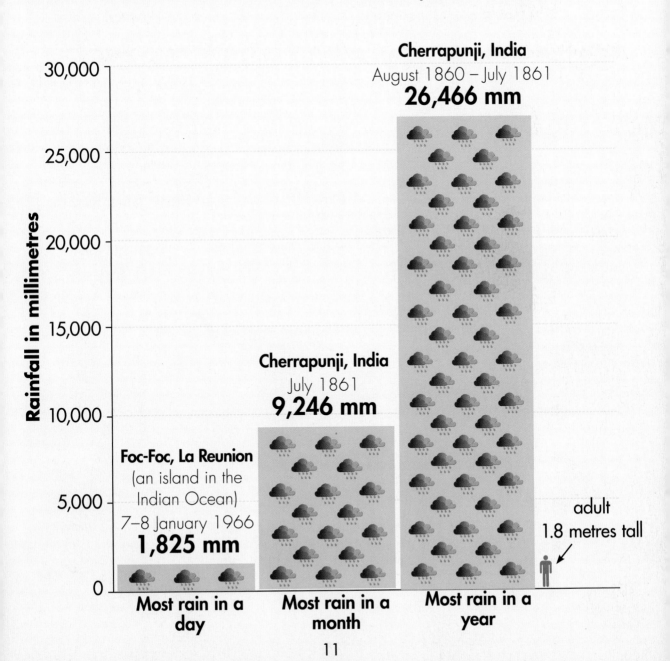

Rainfall in millimetres

- 30,000
- 25,000
- 20,000
- 15,000
- 10,000
- 5,000
- 0

Cherrapunji, India
August 1860 – July 1861
26,466 mm

Cherrapunji, India
July 1861
9,246 mm

Foc-Foc, La Reunion
(an island in the Indian Ocean)
7–8 January 1966
1,825 mm

adult
1.8 metres tall

Most rain in a day

Most rain in a month

Most rain in a year

11

The biggest hail

Hail is made up of lumps of ice that fall from clouds. The lumps are called hailstones. Some hailstones are enormous. This map shows where some of the worst hailstorms have taken place.

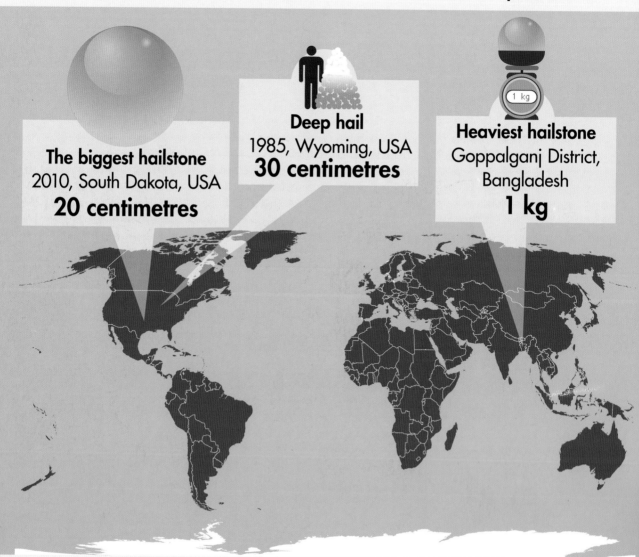

The biggest hailstone
2010, South Dakota, USA
20 centimetres

Deep hail
1985, Wyoming, USA
30 centimetres

Heaviest hailstone
Goppalganj District, Bangladesh
1 kg

1 kg

How snowy?

The amount of snow that falls is measured by how deep the snow gets on the ground. This chart shows the amount of snow that fell each month in Banff, Canada, in 2006.

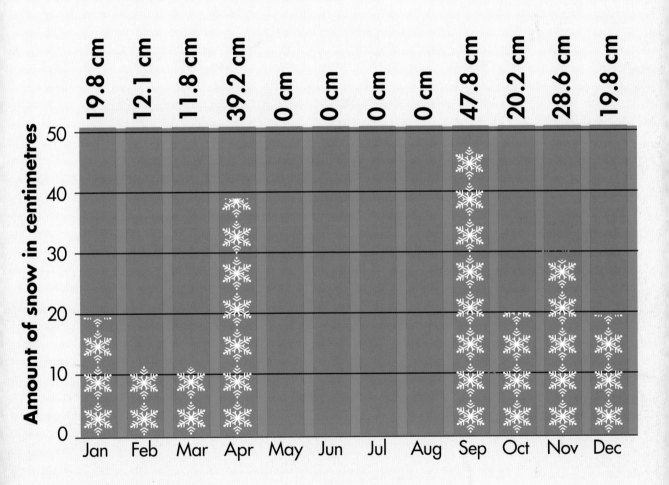

How windy?

Weather experts measure two things about the wind. They measure the strength of the wind and which way the wind is blowing. This chart shows how the strength and direction of the wind at Sydney airport, Australia, changed during a day.

We show wind speed in miles per hour (mph). At **9 am** the strength was **11 mph**

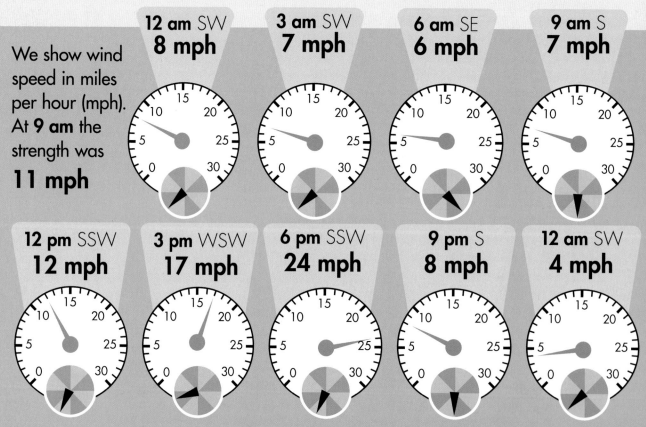

We show wind direction with the points of a **compass**.
At **9 am** the wind was blowing from north to south.

How sunny?

This is an example of a sunshine chart. It shows how many hours of sunshine there was each day for a week.

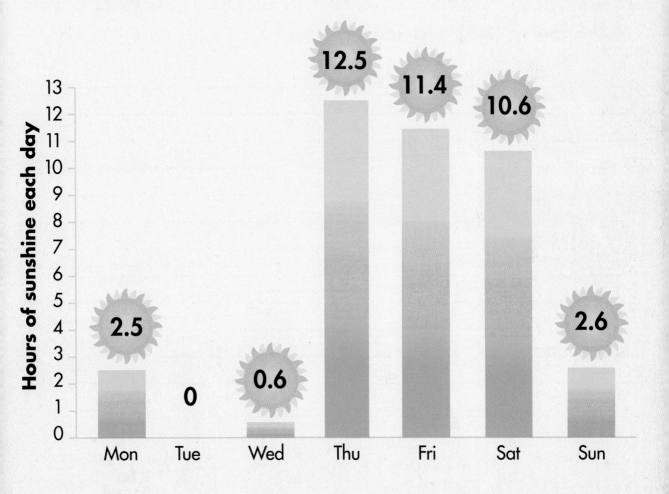

CLOUDS

Cloud shapes and sizes

Clouds come in many different shapes and sizes. This chart shows some of the clouds you might see when you look up into the sky.

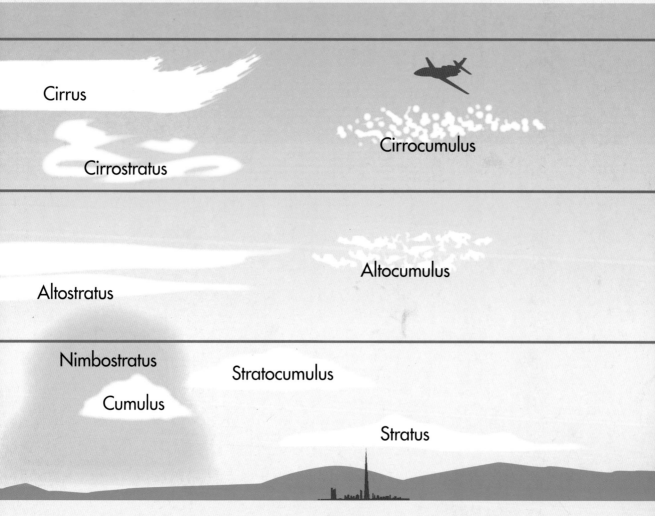

Cirrus

Cirrostratus

Cirrocumulus

Altostratus

Altocumulus

Nimbostratus

Stratocumulus

Cumulus

Stratus

Clouds are named by their shape and how high up in the sky they are.

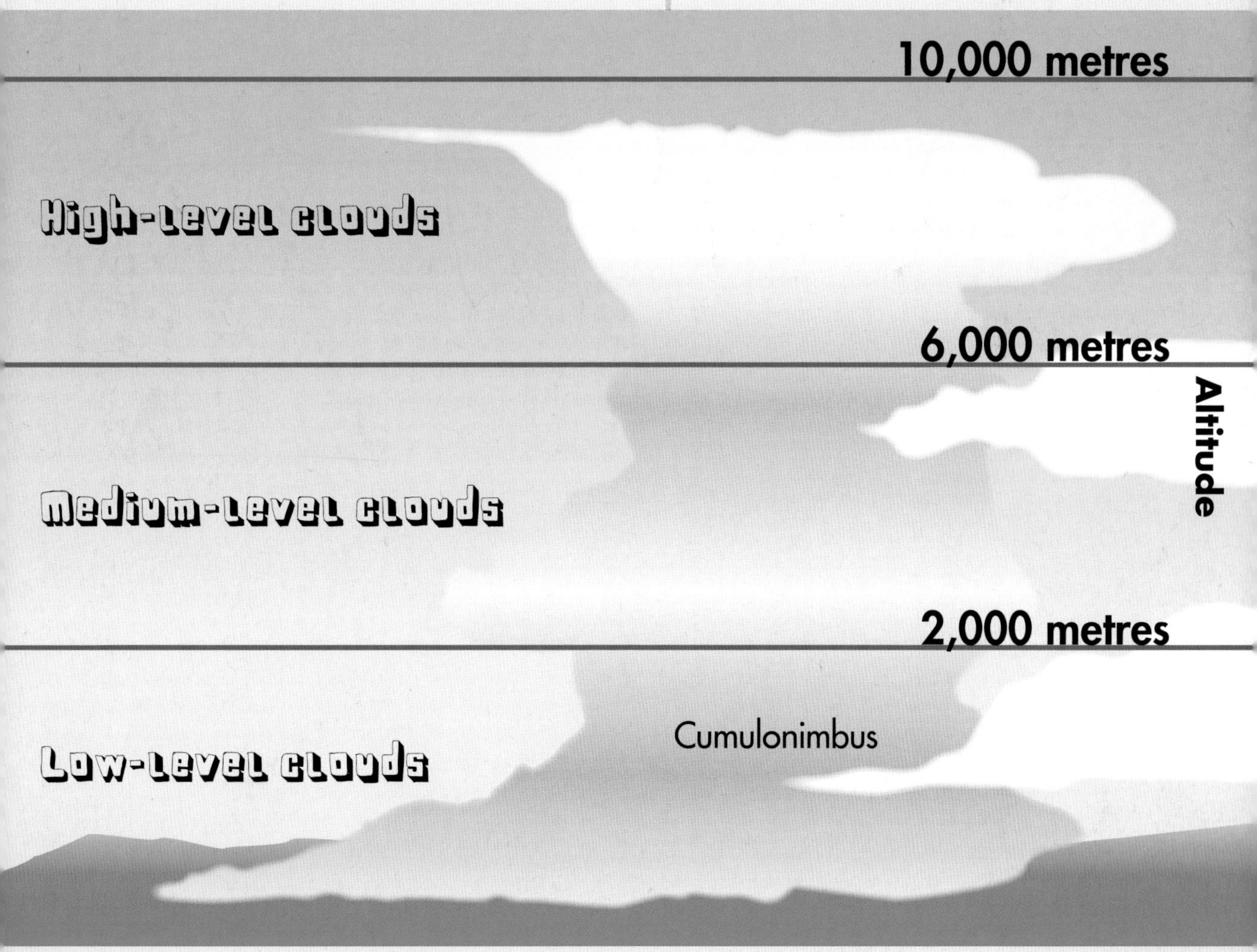

10,000 metres

High-level clouds

6,000 metres

Medium-level clouds

Altitude

2,000 metres

Cumulonimbus

Low-level clouds

Thunder and lightning facts

Thunder storms are giant clouds full of electricity. This infographic is about thunder and **lightning**.

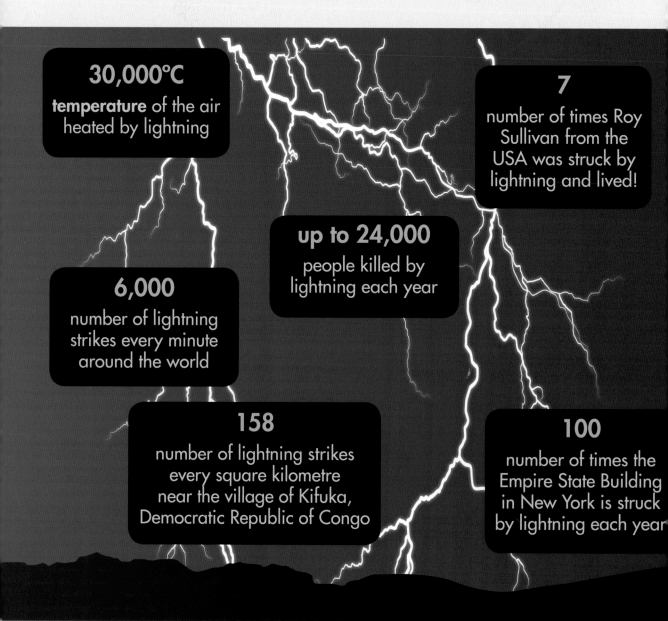

30,000°C
temperature of the air heated by lightning

7
number of times Roy Sullivan from the USA was struck by lightning and lived!

up to 24,000
people killed by lightning each year

6,000
number of lightning strikes every minute around the world

158
number of lightning strikes every square kilometre near the village of Kifuka, Democratic Republic of Congo

100
number of times the Empire State Building in New York is struck by lightning each year

Thunder map

This map shows you which areas of the world get the most thunderstorms.

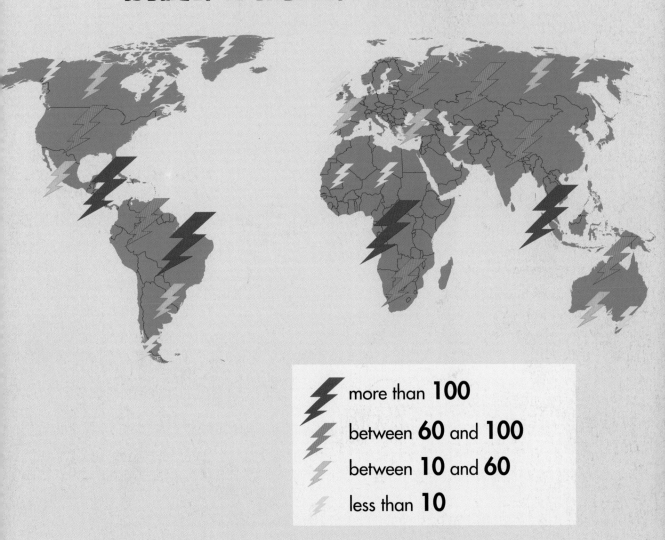

Number of thundery days in a year

more than **100**

between **60** and **100**

between **10** and **60**

less than **10**

EXTREME WEATHER

Hurricanes

A hurricane is a giant swirling storm. Hurricanes start over the sea and sometimes hit land. They can cause terrible destruction. This infographic is about hurricanes.

A hurricane seen from space

bands of cloud

The hole in the middle is called an eye

Hurricane hazards

Very strong winds

Heavy rain

Huge waves

200 kilometres the biggest hurricane eye

1600 kilometres the biggest distance across a

306 kilometres an hour the strongest hurricane winds

Where hurricanes strike

Hurricanes are called cyclones and typhoons in some parts of the world. They form near the equator. This map shows where hurricanes start and the paths they follow.

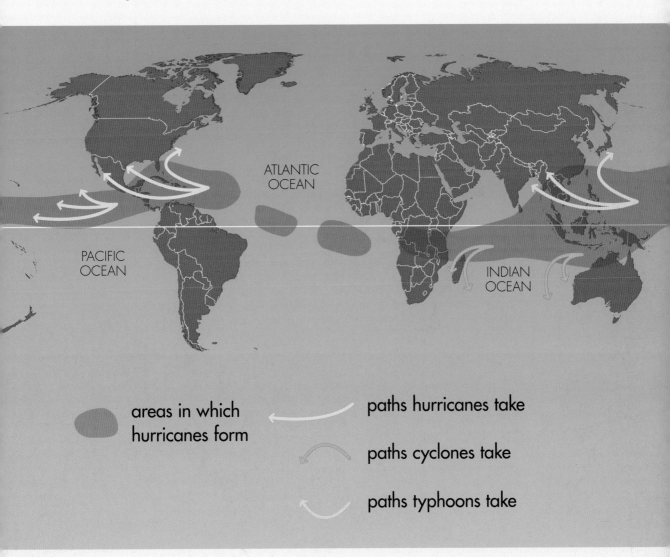

ATLANTIC OCEAN

PACIFIC OCEAN

INDIAN OCEAN

areas in which hurricanes form

paths hurricanes take

paths cyclones take

paths typhoons take

Tornado facts

This infographic is about tornadoes. A tornado is a funnel-shaped storm. It spins very fast, making super-strong winds. Tornadoes always hang down from giant thunderstorms.

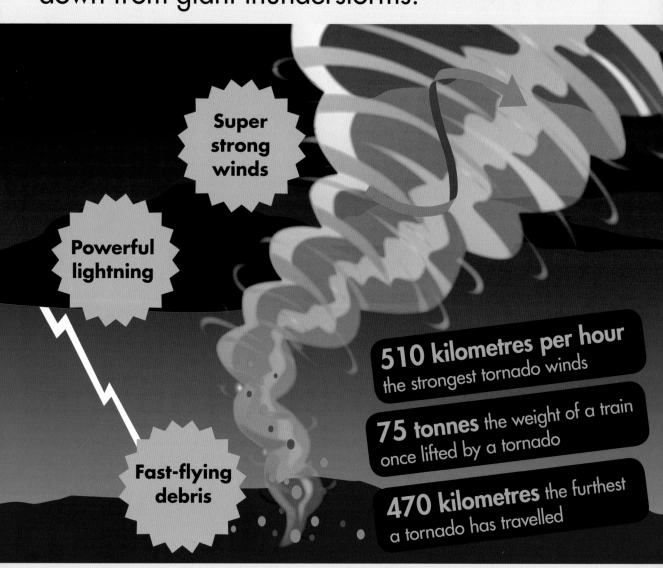

Super strong winds

Powerful lightning

Fast-flying debris

510 kilometres per hour the strongest tornado winds

75 tonnes the weight of a train once lifted by a tornado

470 kilometres the furthest a tornado has travelled

Tornado Alley

Tornadoes happen in many places around the world but the most famous place is an area of the United States known as Tornado Alley. This map shows where Tornado Alley is.

Tornado alley

South Dakota
Minnesota
Iowa
Nebraska
Colorado
Kansas
Oklahoma
Texas

CLIMATES

Climate is the pattern of weather over time. We show climates by how much rain falls during a year, and what the **temperature** is over a year. This chart shows how much rain normally falls each month of the year in a certain place.

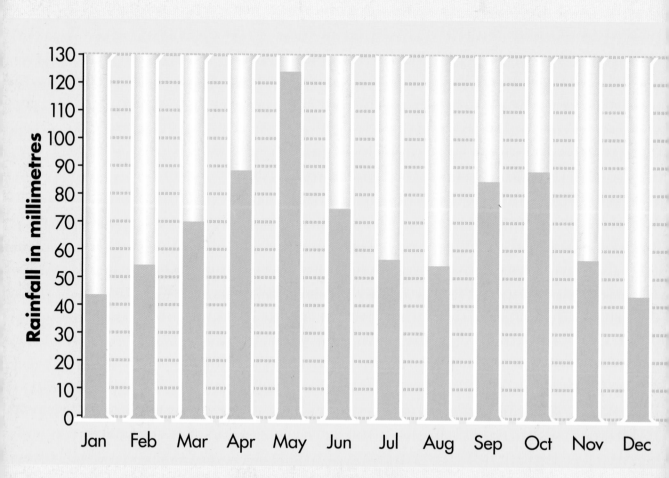

Temperature each month

This line graph shows the **average** temperature in Manchester, UK, for each month for a year. It shows how the temperature rises and falls during the year.

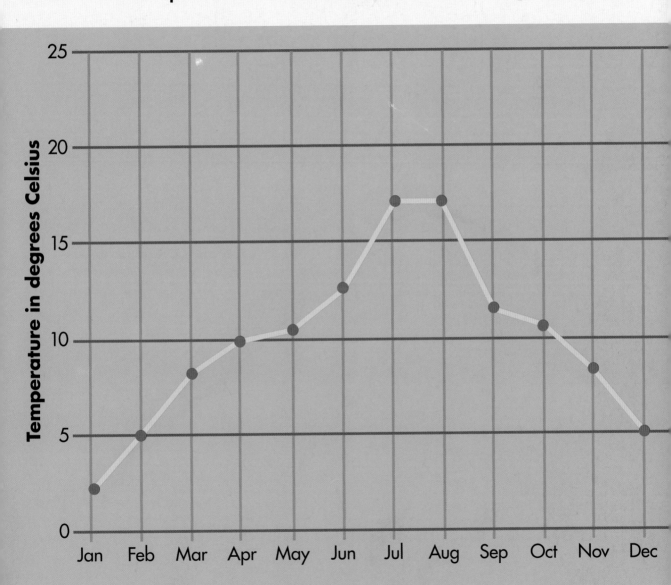

Climates around the world

This map shows what the **climate** is like in different parts of the world.

Polar very cold all year round

Temperate warm summers and cool winters

Desert very dry all year round

Tropical warm and rainy all year round

Mediterranean hot summers and warm winters

Mountains cold and snowy all year round

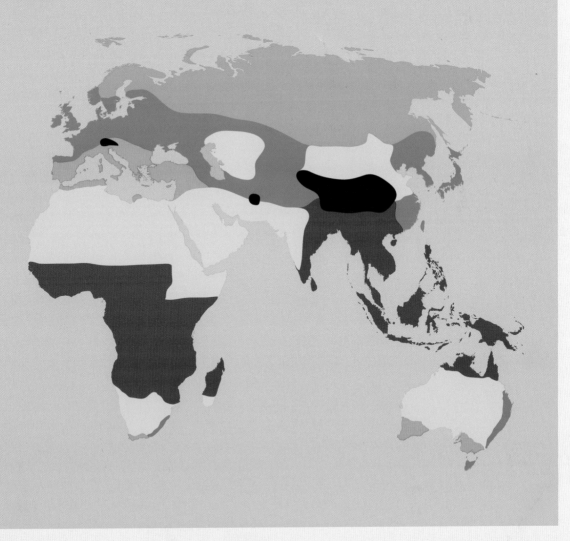

WEATHER FORECASTING

Weather forecasting means working out what the weather might be like for the next few days. This information is shown with weather maps. This is an example of a weather forecast map. You can see what weather will be like where you live.

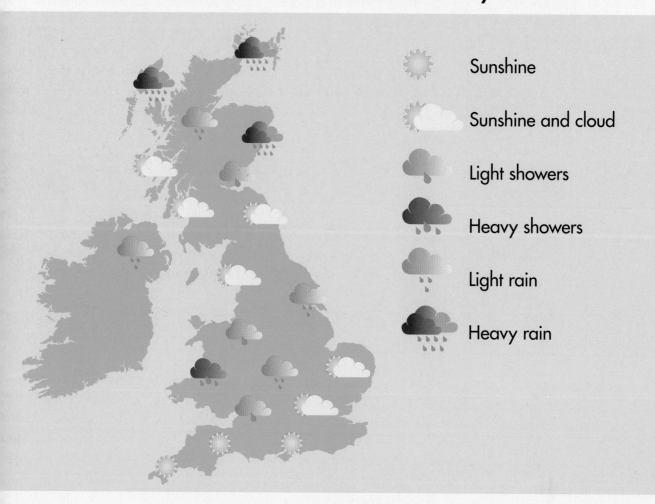

Sunshine

Sunshine and cloud

Light showers

Heavy showers

Light rain

Heavy rain

Weather for the week

This chart is an example of a five-day forecast. It shows in words and pictures what the weather will probably be like in the daytime for the next five days for a particular place.

5 day forecast

Day	Weather	Max. Day (°C)	Min. Night (°C)	Wind (mph)
Mon		28	13	6
Tue		30	15	5
Wed		25	12	8
Thu		23	11	10
Fri		27	14	7

GLOSSARY

average sum of adding a set of numbers together and then dividing by the number of numbers in the set

calm not windy

climate pattern of weather that a place has over a long time

compass instrument for showing direction. A compass has a magnetic needle that points north.

lightning natural electricity produced in thunderclouds. Lightning appears as a bright flash or streak of light in the sky.

temperature how hot or cold something is

thunder booming noise that follows a flash of lightning

FIND OUT MORE

Books

Everything Weather (National Geographic Kids) Kathy Furgang (National Geographic, 2012)

Making Graphs (series), Vijaya Khisty Bodach (Capstone Press, 2008)

Wild Weather (Extreme Nature) Anita Ganeri (Raintree, 2013)

Websites

www.metoffice.gov.uk/education/kids
Find amazing weather facts, games, and much more on this website!

www.nws.noaa.gov/os/reachout/kidspage.shtml
Visit this website to find out about different kinds of extreme weather.

INDEX

climates 24–27
clouds 16–17
cyclones 21

five-day forecasts 5, 29

hail 12
hurricanes 20–21

infographics: what they
    are 4

lightning 18

rainfall 10–11, 24

snow 13
sunshine 15
symbols 6

temperatures 7, 8–9, 25
thunderstorms 18–19,
    22
tornadoes 22–23
typhoons 21

United Kingdom 9, 25
United States 8, 12,
    18, 23

weather forecasting 5,
    28–29
weather maps 28
winds 14, 20, 22
world-record weather 7